The work placement

Suzanne is doing her work experience.
She works every Monday at a fast-food restaurant.
She will tell you all about it.

What to wear

I have to wear a uniform.
It's a white shirt, black trousers,
a waistcoat and black shoes.
Everyone wears the same.
I have to keep it clean myself.

I start work at 9 o'clock.
I try to get there a few minutes early if I can.
Sometimes the bus is late and I get in a flap!

Getting there

Suzanne, have you washe your hands?

Karen is my boss.
She tells me what to do.
She can be quite bossy, but I like her.

This morning I was unpacking the bread rolls and the fries.
Karen is very strict about hygiene.

Breaks & lunchtimes

At 10.45 I can have a short break.
I make myself a cup of tea and sit down.
We have a room where we sit and relax.
Sometimes I talk to the other staff.

After my break, I work in the restaurant.
It is filling up with people.
"Suzanne! The tables in the corner need cleaning!" says Karen.
"Come on! Be as quick as you can!"
I know what to do.

**Firm but polite language
Rude customers**

Someone shouts at me. It's a customer.

"Hey, you! Over here!"

How rude can you get?

He wants some sauce and I go and get it.

I feel cross inside, but I don't say anything.

Next it's the trays.

Some are sticky and dirty.

Karen wants me to clean them.

She hasn't told me how to do it.

Not sure what to do

Now she's on the telephone so I can't ask her.
I ask Martin. He tells me what to do.

At 12 o'clock I have my lunch. Guess what? It's free and we can choose what we want!

Lunchtime

Martin and Janice are a laugh.
They talk to me, the others don't.

After lunch, Karen asks me to sweep the path outside. A boy has just chucked his meal on the ground. What a mess! I don't want to do it.

The nasty jobs

It's freezing outside and it has started to rain.

"Do I have to?" I ask.

"Can't someone else do it?"

"Come on! Cheer up!" Karen says.

"Everyone else is busy!"

I have a moan but I go and do it.

It's time to clear the tables again.
I have a tray full of dirty things in my hands.
"Suzanne!"
Someone has called my name.
I turn my head to see who is calling.

Concentrating on what you are doing

CRASH!

Oh no! I've banged into a customer and dropped the tray on the ground!

I go bright red and say "sorry" over and over again.

Everyone is looking at me.

Karen comes over.

Mishaps and criticism

She looks really cross.

"Come on," she says, "let's get this mess cleared up.

Here's a mop and a bucket."

Janice helps me.

I feel such an idiot!

The mess is cleared up.

It's now 4 o'clock. Time to go.

"Bye, Karen," I say.

"Bye, Suzanne. See you next week."

Is she still cross? I can't tell.

"Bye, Martin! Bye, Janice!" I wave to them.

Friendly staff banter

"Bye, Suzanne. Watch how you go!" says Janice.

"Watch out for lamp posts!" Martin shouts. He's joking, and I laugh.

"Hey, don't you start!" I call back.

Evaluation

How well did Suzanne do?

Do you think she is enjoying her work?

Will Karen be pleased with her?

Do you think it's a nice place to work?

Would you like to work there?